The little
Van Gogh
museum

apples

BASKET OF APPLES, 1887

Oil on canvas
54 x 65 cm
Kröller-Müller Museum, Otterlo

avenue

AVENUE WITH POPLARS IN AUTUMN, 1884

Oil on canvas on panel
98.5 x 66 cm
Van Gogh Museum, Amsterdam

baby

PORTRAIT OF MARCELLE ROULIN, 1888

Oil on canvas
35 x 24 cm
Van Gogh Museum, Amsterdam

bank

BANK OF THE SEINE, 1887

Oil on canvas
32 x 46 cm
Van Gogh Museum, Amsterdam

bat

BAT, 1885

Oil on canvas
41 x 79 cm
Van Gogh Museum, Amsterdam

beach

BEACH WITH PEOPLE STROLLING AND BOATS,
1882 [detail]

Watercolour on paper
27 x 45 cm
Private collection

bed

THE BEDROOM, 1888 [detail]

Oil on canvas
72 x 90 cm
Van Gogh Museum, Amsterdam

bible

billiards

THE NIGHT CAFÉ, 1888 [detail]

Oil on canvas
70 x 89 cm
Yale University Art Gallery, New Haven

blossom

ALMOND BLOSSOM, 1890

Oil on canvas
73.5 x 92 cm
Van Gogh Museum, Amsterdam

boats

**FISHING BOATS ON THE BEACH AT
LES SAINTES-MARIES-DE-LA-MER, 1888**

Oil on canvas
65 x 81.5 cm
Van Gogh Museum, Amsterdam

books

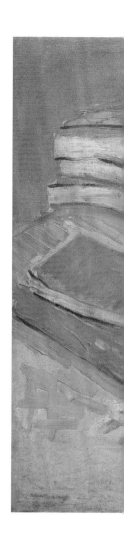

PARISIAN NOVELS, 1888

Oil on canvas
53 x 73.2 cm
Van Gogh Museum, Amsterdam

bow

WOMAN WITH A SCARLET BOW IN HER HAIR, 1885

Oil on canvas
60 x 50 cm
Private collection

boy

PORTRAIT OF CAMILLE ROULIN, 1888

Oil on canvas
40.5 x 32.5 cm
Van Gogh Museum, Amsterdam

bread

STILL LIFE WITH BREAD, 1887

Oil on canvas
32 x 40 cm
Van Gogh Museum, Amsterdam

bridge

**THE LANGLOIS BRIDGE
WITH WASHERWOMEN, 1888**

Oil on canvas
53.4 x 64 cm
Kröller-Müller Museum, Otterlo

bucket

GARDEN OF A BATHHOUSE, 1888 [detail]

Pen on paper
60.7 x 49.2 cm
Van Gogh Museum, Amsterdam

bulbs

BASKET OF HYACINTH BULBS, 1887

Oil on panel (cover of a box)
32 x 48 cm
Van Gogh Museum, Amsterdam

butterflies

BUTTERFLIES AND POPPIES, 1890 [detail]

Oil on canvas
34 cm x 26 cm
Van Gogh Museum, Amsterdam

cabbage

STILL LIFE WITH VEGETABLES AND FRUIT, 1885 [detail]

Oil on canvas
32 x 43 cm
Van Gogh Museum, Amsterdam

candle

GAUGUIN'S CHAIR, 1888 [detail]

Oil on canvas
90.3 x 72.5 cm
Van Gogh Museum, Amsterdam

carriage

THE TARASCON DILIGENCE, 1888

Oil on canvas
72 x 92 cm
Princeton University Art Museum, New Jersey

cat

HAND WITH A BOWL AND A CAT, 1885 [detail]

Black chalk on paper
21 x 35 cm
Van Gogh Museum, Amsterdam

chair

GAUGUIN'S CHAIR, 1888

Oil on canvas
90.3 x 72.5 cm
Van Gogh Museum, Amsterdam

church

CHURCH AT AUVERS, 1890

Oil on canvas
94 x 74 cm
Musée d'Orsay, Paris

city

VIEW OF PARIS, 1886

Oil on canvas
54 x 72.5 cm
Van Gogh Museum, Amsterdam

clogs

PEASANT WOMAN CARRYING WHEAT, 1885 [detail]

Black chalk on paper
58.2 x 38 cm
Kröller-Müller Museum, Otterlo

clouds

WHEAT FIELD UNDER THUNDERCLOUDS, 1890 [detail]

Oil on canvas
50 x 100 cm
Van Gogh Museum, Amsterdam

coffee

THE POTATO EATERS, 1885 [detail]

Oil on canvas
82 x 114 cm
Van Gogh Museum, Amsterdam

cottage

THE COTTAGE, 1885

Oil on canvas
65.7 x 79.3 cm
Van Gogh Museum, Amsterdam

COWS

COWS (AFTER JORDAENS), 1890

Oil on canvas
55 x 65 cm
Musée des Beaux-Arts, Lille

crab

A CRAB ON ITS BACK, 1889

Oil on canvas
38 x 46.5 cm
Van Gogh Museum, Amsterdam

cradle

GIRL KNEELING BY A CRADLE, 1883 [detail]

Pencil, chalk and transparent watercolour on paper
48 x 32.3 cm
Van Gogh Museum, Amsterdam

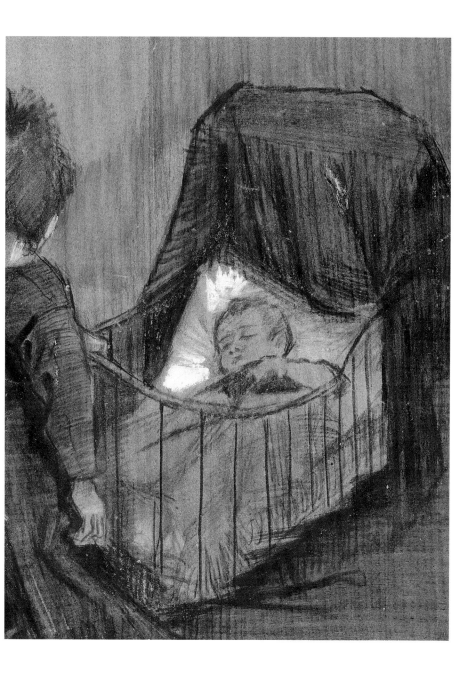

crickets

THREE CICADAS, 1889

Pen and ink on paper
12 x 11 cm
Van Gogh Museum, Amsterdam

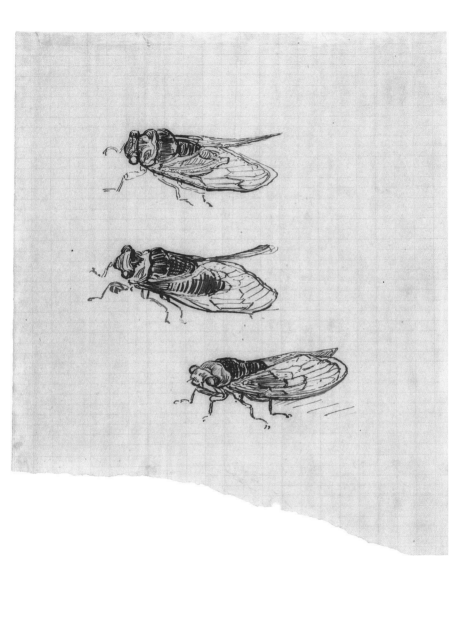

crows

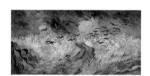

WHEAT FIELD WITH CROWS, 1890 [detail]

Oil on canvas
50.5 x 103 cm
Van Gogh Museum, Amsterdam

cypress

CYPRESSES, 1889

Oil on canvas
95 x 73 cm
The Metropolitan Museum of Art, New York

digging

DIGGERS (AFTER MILLET), 1889

Oil on canvas
72 x 92 cm
Stedelijk Museum, Amsterdam

donkey

MORNING: GOING OUT TO WORK (AFTER MILLET), 1890 [detail]

Oil on canvas
73 x 92 cm
The State Hermitage Museum, Saint Petersburg

drinking

MEN DRINKING (AFTER DAUMIER), 1890

Oil on canvas
60 x 73 cm
The Art Institute of Chicago

factory

FACTORIES AT CLICHY, 1887

Oil on canvas
54 x 72 cm
The Saint Louis Art Museum

fall

FALLING LEAVES ('LES ALYSCAMPS'), 1888

Oil on canvas
72 x 91 cm
Kröller-Müller Museum, Otterlo

fence

**MILLS AT DORDRECHT
(WEESKINDERENDIJK), 1881**

Pencil and chalk on paper
25.5 x 60 cm
Kröller-Müller Museum, Otterlo

field

PLOUGHED FIELDS ('THE FURROWS'), 1888

Oil on canvas
72.5 x 92.5 cm
Van Gogh Museum, Amsterdam

figurine

PLASTER FIGURE OF A FEMALE TORSO, 1887

Oil on canvas
41 x 32 cm
Van Gogh Museum, Amsterdam

fireplace

FIGURES BY THE FIREPLACE, 1890

Chalk on paper
23.5 x 32 cm
Van Gogh Museum, Amsterdam

fountain

FOUNTAIN IN THE GARDEN OF THE ASYLUM, 1889

Chalk, pen and ink on paper
45 x 48 cm
Van Gogh Museum, Amsterdam

frog

COURTESAN (AFTER EISEN), 1887 [detail]

Oil on canvas
105.5 x 60.5 cm
Van Gogh Museum, Amsterdam

garden

DAUBIGNY'S GARDEN, 1890

Oil on canvas
51 x 51 cm
Van Gogh Museum, Amsterdam

girl

ADELINE RAVOUX, 1890

Oil on canvas
71.5 x 53 cm
Present whereabouts unknown

glass

CAFÉ TABLE WITH ABSINTH, 1887 [detail]

Oil on canvas
46.2 x 33.3 cm
Van Gogh Museum, Amsterdam

grapes

GRAPES, 1887

Oil on canvas
32 x 46 cm
Van Gogh Museum, Amsterdam

hands

**THREE HANDS, TWO HOLDING KNIVES,
1884-85**

Black chalk on paper
21.1 x 34.6 cm
Van Gogh Museum, Amsterdam

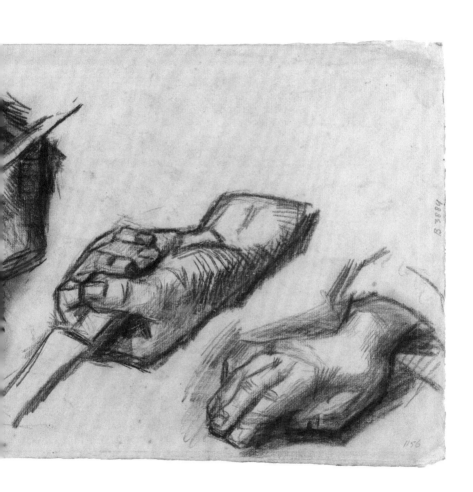

1156

hat

haystack

HAYSTACKS IN PROVENCE, 1888 [detail]

Oil on canvas
73.5 x 93 cm
Kröller-Müller Museum, Otterlo

herring

STILL LIFE WITH HERRINGS, 1889

Oil on canvas
33 x 41 cm
Private collection

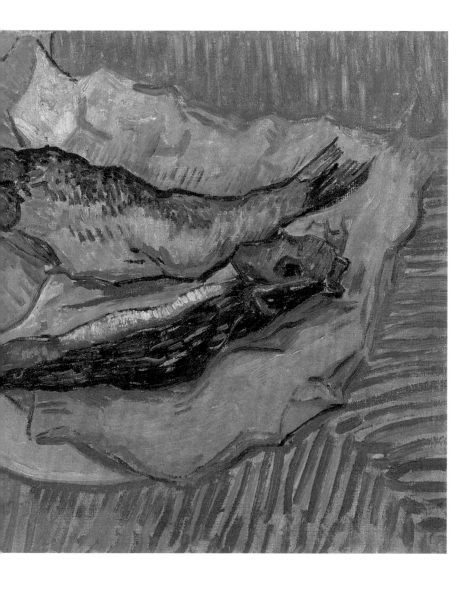

hill

THE HILL OF MONTMARTRE WITH STONE QUARRY, 1886

Oil on canvas
56 x 62 cm
Van Gogh Museum, Amsterdam

horse

HORSE, 1886

Oil on board
33 x 41 cm
Van Gogh Museum, Amsterdam

hospital

WARD IN THE HOSPITAL, 1889

Oil on canvas
74 x 92 cm
Oskar Reinhart Collection, Winterthur

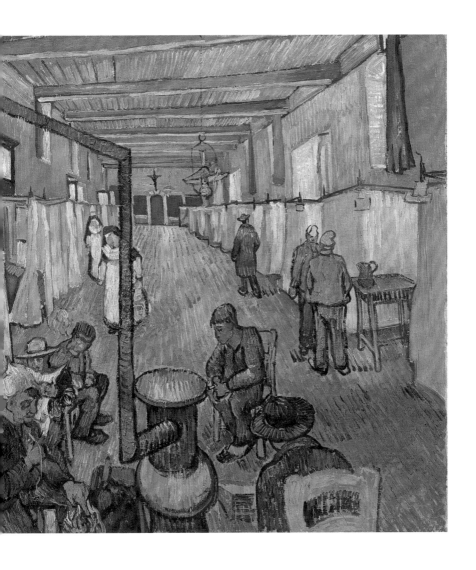

house

THE YELLOW HOUSE ('THE STREET'), 1888

Oil on canvas
72 x 91.5 cm
Van Gogh Museum, Amsterdam

irises

IRISES, 1890

Oil on canvas
92 x 74 cm
Van Gogh Museum, Amsterdam

Jesus

PIETÀ (AFTER DELACROIX), 1889

Oil on canvas
73 x 60.5 cm
Van Gogh Museum, Amsterdam

jug

STILL LIFE WITH BRASS CAULDRON AND JUG, 1885 [detail]

Oil on canvas
65.5 x 80.5 cm
Van Gogh Museum, Amsterdam

kettle

MAN SITTING BY THE FIREPLACE, 1881 [detail]

Chalk and opaque watercolour on paper
55.8 x 44.5 cm
Kröller-Müller Museum, Otterlo

kimono

COURTESAN (**AFTER EISEN**), **1887** [detail]

Oil on canvas
105.5 x 60.5 cm
Van Gogh Museum, Amsterdam

kingfisher

KINGFISHER AT THE WATER'S EDGE, 1887

Oil on canvas
19 x 26 cm
Van Gogh Museum, Amsterdam

knitting

GIRL SITTING, KNITTING, 1882

Pencil on paper
43 x 26.5 cm
Present whereabouts unknown

ladders

HAYSTACKS IN PROVENCE, 1888 [detail]

Oil on canvas
73.5 x 93 cm
Kröller-Müller Museum, Otterlo

lamp

THE POTATO EATERS, 1885 [detail]

Oil on canvas
82 x 114 cm
Van Gogh Museum, Amsterdam

lanterns

VIEW OF THE TERRACE NEAR THE MOULIN DE BLUTE-FIN, 1886

Oil on canvas on panel
44 x 33.5 cm
The Art Institute of Chicago

laundry

CARPENTER'S YARD AND LAUNDRY, 1882 [detail]

Pencil, black chalk, pen, brush and black ink on paper
28.6 x 46.8 cm
Kröller-Müller Museum, Otterlo

lemons

STILL LIFE WITH LEMONS, 1887

Oil on canvas
21 x 26 cm
Van Gogh Museum, Amsterdam

letter

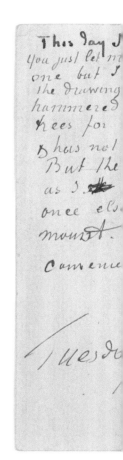

LETTER TO JOHN PETER RUSSELL
ARLES, 17 JUNE 1888

Van Gogh Museum, Amsterdam

to you by bookpost 1 drawing "A Root in a dry ground"
t you think of it. Les Racines is very similar to this
that one neither. "Sorrow" in this manner on a roller
ounted on cardboard. With regard to this one I
single day having studied the same spot and
. So it has been done "tout d'un trait" out of doors
in my studio.
as been slightly damaged in 2 or 3 places
through it. please have this seen to at
t get worse. I think it wants a grey
bye, hope to hear of you at y'early

Vincent

19b

lovers

GARDEN IN MONTMARTRE WITH LOVERS, 1887 [detail]

Oil on canvas
75 x 112.5 cm
Van Gogh Museum, Amsterdam

meal

THE POTATO EATERS, 1885

Oil on canvas
82 x 114 cm
Van Gogh Museum, Amsterdam

mill

MOULIN DE LA GALETTE, 1886

Oil on canvas
38.4 x 46 cm
Kröller-Müller Museum, Otterlo

moon

STARRY NIGHT, 1889 [detail]

Oil on canvas
73 x 92 cm
The Museum of Modern Art, New York

moth

EMPEROR MOTH, 1889

Oil on canvas
33.5 x 24.5 cm
Van Gogh Museum, Amsterdam

nap

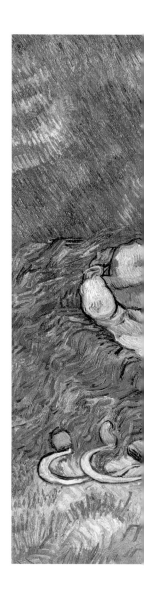

NOON: REST (AFTER MILLET), 1890

Oil on canvas
73 x 91 cm
Musée d'Orsay, Paris

nests

BIRDS' NESTS, 1885

Oil on canvas
39 x 46 cm
Van Gogh Museum, Amsterdam

night

NIGHT (AFTER MILLET), 1889

Oil on canvas
74 x 94 cm
Van Gogh Museum, Amsterdam

nude

FEMALE NUDE, SEEN FROM THE BACK, 1887

Oil on canvas
38 x 61 cm
Private collection

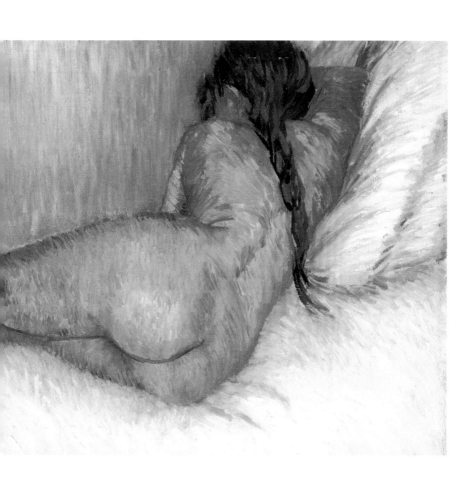

onions

STILL LIFE WITH A PLATE OF ONIONS, 1889 [detail]

Oil on canvas
49.6 x 64.4 cm
Kröller-Müller Museum, Otterlo

oranges

BASKET OF ORANGES, 1888

Oil on canvas
45 x 54 cm
Private collection

orchard

THE WHITE ORCHARD, 1888

Oil on canvas
60 x 81 cm
Van Gogh Museum, Amsterdam

owl

BARN OWL VIEWED FROM THE SIDE, 1887

Pencil, pen and ink on paper
35.3 x 26.2 cm
Van Gogh Museum, Amsterdam

painter

SELF-PORTRAIT AS A PAINTER, 1888

Oil on canvas
65.2 x 50.2 cm
Van Gogh Museum, Amsterdam

pansies

BASKET OF PANSIES, 1886

Oil on canvas
46 x 56 cm
Van Gogh Museum, Amsterdam

parrot

THE GREEN PARROT, 1886

Oil on canvas op panel
48 x 43 cm
Private collection

piano

MARGUERITE GACHET AT THE PIANO, 1890

Oil on canvas
46 x 55 cm
Kunstmuseum Basel

pipe

HEAD OF A MAN, 1885

Oil on canvas
38 x 30 cm
Van Gogh Museum, Amsterdam

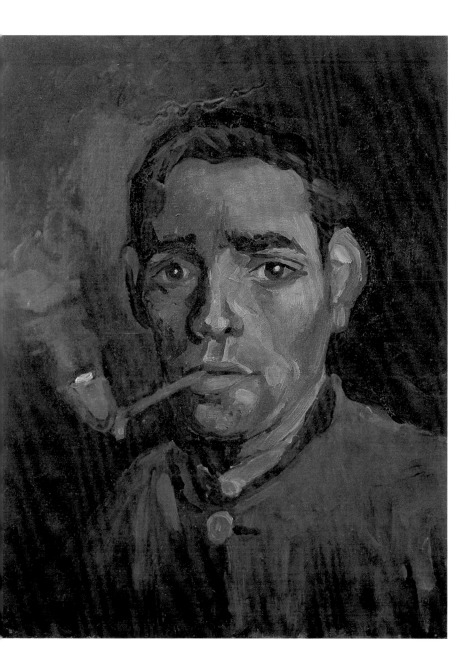

pollard willows

LANDSCAPE WITH PATH AND POLLARD WILLOWS, 1888 [detail]

Pencil, pen and brown ink on paper
26 x 35 cm
Van Gogh Museum, Amsterdam

postman

JOSEPH ROULIN, 1888

Oil on canvas
81 x 65 cm
Museum of Fine Arts, Boston

potatoes

BASKET OF POTATOES, 1885

Oil on canvas
45 x 60 cm
Van Gogh Museum, Amsterdam

prayer

OLD MAN, KNEELING IN PRAYER, 1883

Pencil and black chalk on paper
56 x 46 cm
Present whereabouts unknown

prison

PENITENTIARY (AFTER DORÉ), 1890

Oil on canvas
80 x 64 cm
The Pushkin Museum of Fine Arts, Moscow

190

quarry

OUTSKIRTS OF PARIS NEAR MONTMARTRE, 1887

Gouache, chalk, pencil and ink on paper
39.5 x 53.5 cm
Stedelijk Museum, Amsterdam

quay

QUAY WITH SAND BARGES, 1888

Oil on canvas
55 x 66 cm
Museum Folkwang, Essen

rabbits

LANDSCAPE WITH RABBITS, 1889 [detail]

Oil on canvas
32 x 40 cm
Van Gogh Museum, Amsterdam

rain

BRIDGE IN THE RAIN (AFTER HIROSHIGE), 1887

Oil on canvas
73 x 54 cm
Van Gogh Museum, Amsterdam

reading

MAN, STANDING, READING A BOOK, 1882

Black chalk, pen and ink on paper
64 x 44 cm
Present whereabouts unknown

reaping

THE REAPER (AFTER MILLET), 1889

Oil on canvas
44 x 33 cm
Van Gogh Museum, Amsterdam

restaurant

INTERIOR OF A RESTAURANT, 1887

Oil on canvas
45.5 x 56 cm
Kröller-Müller Museum, Otterlo

rocks

THE ROCK OF MONTMAJOUR WITH PINE TREES, 1888

Pencil, pen and ink on paper
49 x 61 cm
Van Gogh Museum, Amsterdam

roofs

VIEW FROM VINCENT'S STUDIO, 1886

Oil on board
30 x 41 cm
Van Gogh Museum, Amsterdam

roses

ROSES AND PEONIES, 1886

Oil on canvas
59.8 x 72.5 cm
Kröller-Müller Museum, Otterlo

sea

**SEASCAPE NEAR
LES SAINTES-MARIES-DE-LA-MER, 1888**

Oil on canvas
64.3 x 50.5 cm
Van Gogh Museum, Amsterdam

shepherd

SHEPHERD WITH FLOCK OF SHEEP, 1884

Oil on canvas on board
67 x 126 cm
Soumaya Museum, Mexico City

shoes

SHOES, 1886

Oil on canvas
37.5 x 45 cm
Van Gogh Museum, Amsterdam

shrimps

SHRIMPS AND MUSSELS, 1886

Oil on canvas
27 x 34 cm
Van Gogh Museum, Amsterdam

skull

SKULL OF A SKELETON WITH A BURNING CIGARETTE, 1886

Oil on canvas
32 x 24 cm
Van Gogh Museum, Amsterdam

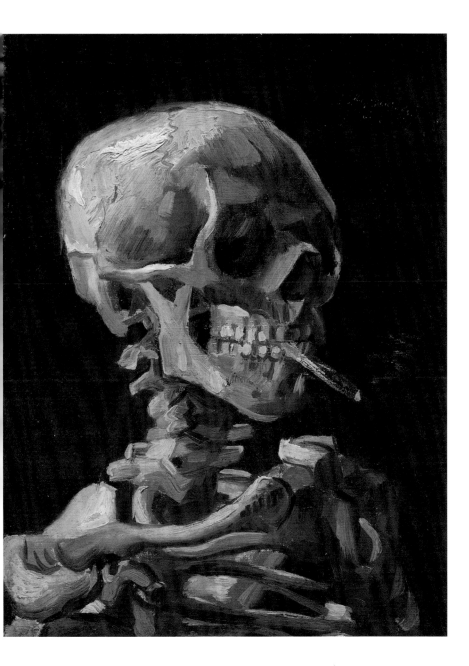

snow

LANDSCAPE WITH SNOW, 1888

Oil on canvas
38 x 46 cm
The Solomon R. Guggenheim Museum, New York

sorrow

SORROW, 1882

Lithograph
38.5 x 29 cm
Van Gogh Museum, Amsterdam

Vincent

Sorrow

1ᵉ epreuve

sowing

THE SOWER (AFTER MILLET), 1881

Pencil, ink and watercolour on paper
48.1 x 36.7 cm
Van Gogh Museum, Amsterdam

sprig

SPRIG OF FLOWERING ALMOND BLOSSOM IN A GLASS, 1888

Oil on canvas
24 x 19 cm
Van Gogh Museum, Amsterdam

stairs

THE TRINQUETAILLE BRIDGE, 1888

Oil on canvas
73.5 x 92.5 cm
Present whereabouts unknown

stars

STARRY NIGHT OVER THE RHÔNE, 1888

Oil on canvas
72.5 x 92 cm
Musée d'Orsay, Paris

sun

SOWER, 1888 [detail]

Oil on canvas
32 x 40 cm
Van Gogh Museum, Amsterdam

sunflowers

SUNFLOWERS, 1889

Oil on canvas
95 x 73 cm
Van Gogh Museum, Amsterdam

terrace

TERRACE OF A CAFÉ AT NIGHT (PLACE DU FORUM), 1888

Oil on canvas
80.7 x 65.3 cm
Kröller-Müller Museum, Otterlo

thistles

THISTLES, 1888

Oil on canvas
59 x 49 cm
Private collection

tired

**MAN SITTING BY THE FIREPLACE
('WORN OUT'), 1881**

Pen and watercolour on paper
23.5 x 31 cm
P. & N. de Boer Foundation, Amsterdam

tower

THE OLD CHURCH TOWER AT NUENEN ('THE PEASANTS' CHURCHYARD'), 1885

Oil on canvas
65 x 80 cm
Van Gogh Museum, Amsterdam

tree

THE PINK PEACH TREE, 1888

Oil on canvas
80.5 x 59 cm
Van Gogh Museum, Amsterdam

tunnel

THE VIADUCT, 1887

Oil on board on panel
33 x 40.5 cm
The Solomon R. Guggenheim Museum, New York

village

**VIEW OF LES SAINTES-MARIES-DE-LA-MER,
1888** [detail]

Oil on canvas
64.2 x 53 cm
Kröller-Müller Museum, Otterlo

wagon

THE HARVEST, 1888 [detail]

Oil on canvas
73 x 92 cm
Van Gogh Museum, Amsterdam

water mill

THE WATER MILL IN GENNEP, 1884

Oil on canvas
60 x 78.5 cm
Instituut Collectie Nederland, on permanent loan
to Noord-Brabants Museum, Den Bosch

weaving

WEAVER AND A SPINNING WHEEL, 1884

Oil on canvas
61 x 85 cm
Museum of Fine Arts, Boston

wheat

EARS OF WHEAT, 1890

Oil on canvas
64 x 48 cm
Van Gogh Museum, Amsterdam

wheat field

WHEAT FIELD WITH A REAPER, 1889

Oil on canvas
74 x 92 cm
Van Gogh Museum, Amsterdam

window

WINDOW IN THE STUDIO, 1889

Chalk and opaque watercolour on paper
61 x 47 cm
Van Gogh Museum, Amsterdam

wine

STILL LIFE WITH WINE, BREAD AND CHEESE, 1886 [detail]

Oil on canvas
37.5 x 46 cm
Van Gogh Museum, Amsterdam

wood

WOOD WITH COPPICE, 1887

Oil on canvas
46 x 56 cm
Van Gogh Museum, Amsterdam

woodcutter

THE WOODCUTTER (AFTER MILLET), 1889

Oil on canvas
44 x 26.2 cm
Van Gogh Museum, Amsterdam

The life of

Vincent
van Gogh

Vincent van Gogh at age 13

———————

Vincent Willem van Gogh was born in Zundert in North Brabant
on 30 March 1853. He left school when he was sixteen and went to work
in The Hague as an office boy for the art dealers Goupil & Cie.
Later he worked for them in London and Paris as well,
because he had learned English and French at school.
At first Vincent really liked his job. He learned a lot about art
and saw the most wonderful paintings and drawings,
but after a year or two he did not enjoy his work any more.
His employers in Paris noticed that too, and in 1876 they dismissed him.

Vincent van Gogh at age 19

After this Vincent had various other jobs. For example, he worked
as an assistant teacher in England and as a bookseller in Dordrecht.
For a while he preached to the coal miners in the Borinage in Belgium,
teaching them about God and the Bible. Vincent did not do very well
at any of these jobs. He was always looking for something different,
but he did not really know what he wanted to do.

Theo van Gogh, 1882

It was Vincent's younger brother Theo who brought about a great change.
Vincent often made little drawings in the letters that he wrote, and Theo
suggested that he should do something with them. Vincent took his advice:
in 1880 he decided that he would become an artist. Theo had a good job,
so he was able to make sure that Vincent had enough money to live on.
This meant Vincent could concentrate on his art.

The potato eaters, 1885

You do not become an artist overnight, so at first Vincent practised
by making a lot of drawings. After a year or two he began painting. In 1885
he made *The potato eaters*, the painting that he regarded as his first master-
piece. Hardly anyone else agreed with him, though. A lot of people did not
like the dark colours and the figures. One of Vincent's friends even wrote,
'why must the woman on the left have a sort of little pipe stem
with a cube on it for a nose?'

Self-portrait, 1887

In 1886 Vincent went back to Paris, where he saw paintings by French artists that were not like anything he was used to. These pictures made Vincent change his style of painting. For instance, he started to use far more colours, which were also much lighter. In 1888 he went to the south of France, where he found many good subjects to paint.

The yellow house ('The street'), 1888

Vincent found a house where he could live and work in a place called Arles.
At first he really enjoyed being there. He often went out into the countryside
to paint. Unfortunately, it was also in Arles that Vincent suffered
for the first time from an illness that sometimes left him badly confused.
At those moments he did not know exactly what he was doing.
After a while, at his own request, he was admitted to a mental hospital.
There he was able to spend most of his time painting.

Wheat field under thunderclouds, 1890

After a year, when he was feeling better, Vincent went to Auvers-sur-Oise near Paris. Again he worked hard, but he was afraid that his illness would come back. On 27 July 1890 he went out into a wheat field and shot himself in the chest. He died two days later with Theo at his side.

Vincent had worked as an artist for ten years.

Altogether he made about 850 paintings and almost 1,300 drawings.

Van Gogh Museum, Amsterdam

Only a few people understood Vincent's work during his lifetime.
Things are very different now: Vincent van Gogh is world famous.
A lot of his work can be found in the Van Gogh Museum in Amsterdam,
where there are more than 200 paintings, including masterpieces like
The potato eaters of 1885, *Self-portrait as an artist* of 1887, *The yellow house ('The
street')* of 1888, *Sunflowers* of 1889 and *Wheat field under thunderclouds* of 1890.
The Van Gogh Museum also has almost 500 drawings and 800 letters
by Vincent. These works show us that Vincent van Gogh was
one of the greatest painters of the nineteenth century.

**You can find more information about Vincent van Gogh
and the Van Gogh Museum at
www.vangoghmuseum.nl**

The little
Van Gogh
museum

This book is published in cooperation with the Van Gogh Museum Amsterdam.

Editorial advice by
René van Blerk
Suzanne Bogman
Hans Luijten
Anja Wisseborn

Image assistance by
Mariëlle Gerritsen
Femke Grutter
Maria Smit

Text 'The life of Vincent van Gogh' by
René van Blerk

Translations from Dutch by
Lynne Richards

Typesetting and design by
quod. voor de vorm.

Printed by
Indice, Barcelona

© 2010 Ludion, Antwerp

www.ludion.be
www.vangoghmuseum.nl

ISBN: 978-90-5544-956-9
D/2010/6328/59